Getting Started
with
dBase III Plus™

John Wiley & Sons Publishers

New York   Chichester   Brisbane   Toronto   Singapore

CONTENTS

INTRODUCING dBASE III PLUS

General Information 2
Limitations 3
Starting Up dBASE III PLUS 3
Menu Screen Components 4
ASSIST Mode 6
DOT Mode 6
Function Keys 6
Exit dBASE III PLUS 7
Review Questions 8

LESSON 1

Data Base Management 9
Help Facility 10
Setting the Default Drive 11
Creating a File in ASSIST 12
Display Record Structure 15
Add New Records - Append 15
Creating a File in DOT Prompt 16
Making a Backup Copy 18
Saving a File 19
Review Questions 20

LESSON 2

Modify Command 21
Retrieve File in ASSIST 21
Add a Field to Structure 21
Modify Field Structure 22
Change Record Contents 23
List Records 25
Retrieve File in DOT Prompt 28
Display Data 28
Review Questions 32

Lesson 3

Change Record Contents 33
Replace Records 34
Replacing Fields 35
Statistical Functions 37
Arithmetic 38
DOT Prompt History Feature 39

Lesson 4

Sorting Files in ASSIST 40
Sorting Files in DOT Prompt 42
Creating Index 43

Lesson 5

Retrieving a File With Index 46
Browse - Append 47
Browse - Edit 48
Edit in DOT Prompt 49
Deleting Records and Files 50
Delete Single Record 50
Delete Multiple Records 52
Delete a File 52
Review Questions 53

Lesson 6

Joining Database Files 54
Join All Fields 54
Join Selected Fields 55
Creating Reports 56
Report Format - Headings 56
Report Format - Columns 56
Retrieving Report Format 57
Review Questions 58

EXHIBIT "A"

Important: Please read this page before using the dBASE III PLUS program, a copy of which is being made available to you for use in conjunction with the Textbook pursuant to the terms of this Agreement for educational, training and/or demonstration purposes. By using the dBASE III PLUS program, you show your agreement to the terms of this license.

EXCLUSIONS OF WARRANTIES AND LIMITATIONS OF LIABILITY

THE COPY OF THE dBASE III PLUS PROGRAM MADE AVAILABLE FOR USE WITH THIS TEXTBOOK IS A LIMITED FUNCTIONALITY VERSION OF dBASE III PLUS, AND IS INTENDED SOLELY FOR EDUCATIONAL, TRAINING AND DEMONSTRATION PURPOSES. ACCORDINGLY, THIS COPY OF dBASE III PLUS IS PROVIDED "AS IS," WITHOUT WARRANTY OF ANY KIND FROM ASHTON-TATE OR JOHN WILEY & SONS, INC. ASHTON-TATE AND JOHN WILEY & SONS, INC. HEREBY DISCLAIM ALL WARRANTIES OF ANY KIND WITH RESPECT TO THIS LIMITED FUNCTIONALITY COPY OF dBASE III PLUS, INCLUDING WITHOUT LIMITATION THE IMPLIED WARRANTIES OF MERCHANTABILITY AND FITNESS FOR A PARTICULAR PURPOSE. NEITHER ASHTON-TATE NOR JOHN WILEY & SONS, INC. SHALL BE LIABLE UNDER ANY CIRCUMSTANCES FOR CONSEQUENTIAL, INCIDENTAL, SPECIAL OR EXEMPLARY DAMAGES ARISING OUT OF THE USE OF THIS LIMITED FUNCTIONALITY COPY OF dBASE III PLUS, EVEN IF ASHTON-TATE OR JOHN WILEY & SONS, INC. HAS BEEN APPRISED OF THE LIKELIHOOD OF SUCH DAMAGES OCCURRING. IN NO EVENT WILL ASHTON-TATE'S OR JOHN WILEY & SONS, INC.'S LIABILITY (WHETHER BASED ON AN ACTION OR CLAIM IN CONTRACT, TORT OR OTHERWISE) ARISING OUT OF THE USE OF THIS LIMITED FUNCTIONALITY COPY OF dBASE III PLUS EXCEED THE AMOUNT PAID FOR THIS TEXTBOOK.

LIMITED USE SOFTWARE LICENSE AGREEMENT

DEFINITIONS

The term "Software" as used in this agreement means the Limited Use version of dBASE III PLUS which is made available for use in conjunction with this Textbook solely for educational, training and/or demonstration purposes. The term "Software Copies" means the actual copies of all or any portion of the Software, including back-ups, updates, merged or partial copies permitted hereunder.

PERMITTED USES

You may:

-- Load into RAM and use the Software on a single terminal or a single workstation of a computer (or its replacement).

-- Install the Software onto a permanent storage device (a hard disk drive).

-- Make and maintain up to three back up copies provided they are used only for back-up purposes, and you keep possession of the back-ups. In addition, all the information appearing on the original disk labels (including copyright notice) must be copied onto the back-up labels.

This license gives you certain limited rights to use the Software and Software Copies for educational, training and/or demonstration purposes. You do not become the owner of and Ashton-Tate retains title to, all the Software and Software Copies. In addition, you agree to use reasonable efforts to protect the Software from unauthorized use, reproduction, distribution or publication.

All rights not specifically granted in this license are reserved by Ashton-Tate.

USES NOT PERMITTED

You may not:

-- Make copies of the Software, except as permitted above.

-- Rent, lease, sublicense, time-share, lend or transfer the Software, Software Copies or your rights under this license except that transfers may be made with Ashton-Tate's prior written authorization.

-- Alter, decompile, disassemble, or reverse-engineer the Software.

-- Remove or obscure the Ashton-Tate copyright and trademark notices.

-- Use the Software or Software Copies outside the United States or Canada.

DURATION

This agreement is effective from the day you first use the Software. Your license continues for fifty years or until you return to Ashton-Tate the original disks and any back-up copies, whichever comes first.

If you breach this agreement, Ashton-Tate can terminate this license upon notifying you in writing. You will be required to return all Software Copies. Ashton-Tate can also enforce our other legal rights.

GENERAL

This agreement represents the entire understanding and agreement regarding the Software and Software. Copies and supersedes any prior purchase order, communication, advertising or representation.

This license may only be modified in a written amendment signed by an authorized Ashton-Tate officer. If any provision of this agreement shall be unlawful, void, or for any reason unenforceable, it shall be deemed severable from, and shall in no way affect the validity or enforceability of the remaining provisions of this agreement. This agreement will be governed by California law.

INTRODUCING
dBASE III PLUS™

Hardware Needed:
IBM or IBM compatible microcomputer
Dual floppy disk drives or hard drive with one
    floppy disk drive

Software Needed:
PC-DOS or MS-DOS 2.0 or later version
dBASE III PLUS Limited Use Version
Work Disk
Student Data Disk

GENERAL INFORMATION

In this tutorial, you will go through the basic dBASE III PLUS commands using the ASSIST and DOT modes. It may be necessary for you to repeat parts of this tutorial in order to fully master each command and idea.

Most of the ASSIST commands and procedures you will be following will allow you to create databases, enter data for them, store, retrieve and/or manipulate this database information. You will probably be working from dBASE III PLUS on drive C (C:\>) on a fixed disk or B drive (B:\>) if using two floppy disk drives. Your data disk will most likely be in drive A (A:\>). This is a distinction you should keep in mind as you progress through the tutorial. If you have difficulty running the program or finding your database data, you should check to see that you are on the appropriate disk drive.

Before you begin to create databases and store data in them, REMEMBER that the information will exist in two places: on disk, and in the computer's memory. If you want to permanently save the information, you must save the information to disk and exit from dBASE III PLUS properly. If you don't follow those steps, you may be forced to repeat some or all of the tutorial in order to complete and save the work. The plan of this tutorial is to let you try several things, stop and REVIEW, and give you some review questions to check your grasp of the essentials.

The format of the commands described in this material is as follows: All entries to be made by you are printed in **BOLD, CAPITAL LETTERS**. To improve the appearance of alphabetic data we recommend that you keep the [CapsLock] key locked in upper case, unless you specifically want lower case text.

This tutorial will take you through the basic dBASE III PLUS operations beginning with starting your program. (You have already learned how to start your PC in the DOS tutorial.) At the beginning, most of what you will do will consist of Menu choice instructions for creating files, entering data into them, and using that data in specific ways. Gradually, as your understanding and ability develops in using this software, the menu approach of creating commands will give way to your typing the specific commands to save time.

The lessons, with objectives, are divided into six sections:

1)   Creating a File and Entering Records in dBASE III PLUS;

2)   Retrieving a File and Modifying the Record Contents and Structure;

3) Replacing and Listing Records;

4) Sorting and Indexing Records;

5) Appending, Editing, and Deleting Records; and

6) Joining Databases and Printing Customized Reports.

Limitations

The Limited Use version of dBASE III PLUS is restricted to 31 records. Otherwise, all commands and functions are fully operational. Additionally, the message of "(DEMO)" will appear on the screen when using the DOT prompt mode of entering commands.

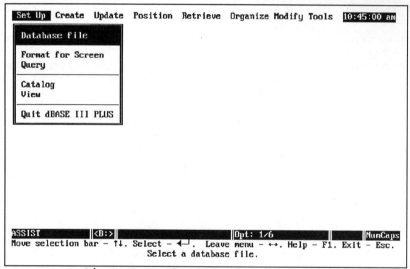

Figure I-1: dBASE III PLUS Beginning

Starting up dBASE III PLUS

LOAD THE dBASE III PLUS SOFTWARE
There are four steps in loading dBASE III PLUS!

Hard Disk Drive

If you are using a hard disk with dBASE III PLUS stored on the disk:

1. Power on the computer to the C:\> prompt.
2. Insert your data disk in drive A and close the door.

DBASE	3. Type **DBASE** at the C:\> prompt (or whichever subdirectory you use to hold the dBASE III PLUS program).
[Enter]	4. Press **[Enter]** key.

You are now ready to begin using dBASE III PLUS when Figure I-1 appears.

Floppy Disk Drives

If you are using two floppy disk drives:

	1. Power on the computer to the B:\> prompt.
	2. Insert your disk #1 in drive B and close the door.
DBASE [Enter]	3. Type **DBASE** at the B:\> prompt and press the **[Enter]** key.
[Enter]	4. Replace disk #1 with disk #2 and press the **[Enter]** key.
	5. Insert your data disk in drive A and close the door.

You are now ready to begin using dBASE III PLUS when Figure I-1 appears.

The Menu Screen Components

Study Figure I-2. Each of the referenced areas is explained below.

1.	Menu Bar	The main menu bar consists of current operation headings. Use the [←], [→] keys and [Enter], or the first letter of the command and [Enter] to move to a particular heading.
2.	Submenu	The pulldown menu contains the list of choices under a menu heading. Each main menu heading has its own submenu.
3.	Clock Display	The clock display gives the current time. If your computer has a battery powered clock, or you have set the time in DOS, the current time will appear. Otherwise the clock will begin when the software is booted.
4.	Action Line	This line indicates the command that is being created by your menu choice or typed in through the DOT prompt mode. At present it is blank because no command has been issued.

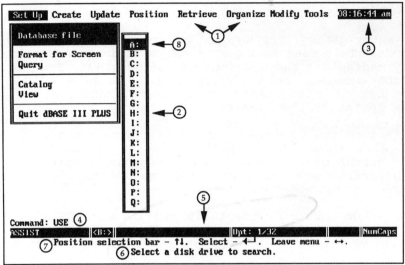

Figure I-2:   Screen Components

5.   Status Bar   The Status bar has six sections that display information about the current status of the program:

     A.   Mode - This shows the current mode, one of three; (1) ASSIST, (2) Command Line (DOT prompt), or (3) Command (Programming).

     B.   Drive - Indicates which disk drive has been selected to access data files.

     C.   File - Indicates the data file that is currently is use.

     D.   Location - Position of the pointer in the file and total number of records in the file.

     E.   Insert/Overtype - Indicates status of typing of either insert mode or overtype mode.

     F.   Locks - Indicates whether the CapsLock and Numlock keys have been activated.

6.   Message Line   The message line displays information about the current command.

7.   Navigation Line   A message line requiring an option selection or displays an error explanation.

8.   Selection Bar   The highlighted area on the main menu or within a submenu.

5

ASSIST Mode

When you enter dBASE III PLUS, you are automatically placed in the ASSIST mode. This mode is a series of menus designed to enable you to easily manipulate the commands of the program. You can move to any of the commands on the main menu line by positioning the selection bar on that command and pressing [Enter] or by pressing the first letter of the command.

After selecting the command to use from the main menu, one or more submenus will appear with specific action options. This menu approach should permit you to achieve your specific goal with minimal effort. The alternative to the menu approach is called the DOT prompt command mode.

If the DOT mode should accidentally replace the ASSIST mode while you are working at the terminal, you can easily move back to the ASSIST mode by typing **ASSIST** and pressing **[Enter]** or press **[F2]**.

DOT Prompt Mode

Another mode of dBASE III PLUS operation also exists, called the DOT prompt, because its prompt is a period (DOT). This mode is command-line oriented, meaning that you type commands when you are at the DOT prompt. Press the [Esc] key to use the DOT prompt mode.

The DOT prompt puts you in command mode where you can do some things that are not available from the ASSIST mode. Also, it allows you to do some things faster than selecting from menus, if you know the command to use. It is also important because the commands that are entered from the DOT prompt can be placed together in a program, to allow the user to perform complicated and specific user-defined applications.

Function Keys

The function keys are located either on the left side of the main keyboard or across the top. The function keys that can be used are indicated by an F preceding the numbers 1 through 10.

The commands that these particular programmable keys are already set for are the following:

[F2] – ASSIST	[F7] – DISPLAY MEMORY
[F3] – LIST	[F8] – DISPLAY
[F4] – DIR	[F9] – APPEND
[F5] – DISPLAY STRUCTURE	[F10] – EDIT
[F6] – DISPLAY STATUS	

The function keys are especially useful when using the DOT prompt commands.

Exit dBASE III PLUS

There are two ways to exit dBASE III PLUS: (1) from the ASSIST menu mode and (2) from the DOT prompt mode.

When you are in the ASSIST mode, select the **Set Up** menu and position the cursor to highlight the **Quit dBASE III PLUS** option as shown in Figure I-3 and press **[Enter]**. You are returned to the DOS prompt.

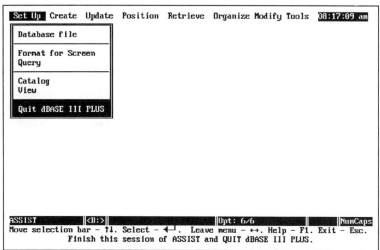

Figure I-3: Quit dBASE III PLUS

To exit dBASE III PLUS from the DOT prompt:

> Type **QUIT [Enter]**
>> You are returned to the DOS prompt.

Use either one of these methods to exit to the DOS prompt.

WARNING

Wait until the DOS prompt appears before turning off the computer.

> Turn off the computer.
>
> Remove your work disk from drive A.
>
> Safely store your work disk. You will use it in later lessons.

7

Summary

You have learned how to start dBASE III PLUS and switch between the ASSIST menu and the DOT prompt modes. The software has some built in functions accessible through the function keys. The keys are especially useful in the DOT prompt mode. Finally, you learned there are two ways to exit dBASE III PLUS properly. It is important to use one of the two methods to safely close all files. Failure to close the files before turning the computer off can result in lost of data!

REVIEW QUESTIONS

1. What should you do to start up dBASE III PLUS?

2. What should you do to quit or exit the program?

3. What should you do to return to the ASSIST mode from the DOT command mode?

4. What DOT command should you use to return to the DOS prompt?

5. Which function key do you use to switch from the DOT prompt mode to the ASSIST mode?

6. Which key do you use to switch from the ASSIST mode to the DOT prompt?

LESSON 1
Creating a File
and Entering Records in
dBASE III PLUS

After completing this lesson, you will be able to:
o   **Understand the purpose of a data base**
o   **Use the Help facility**
o   **Create a data base file**
o   **Create a record field structure**
o   **Append records**
o   **List data entries in the file**
o   **Display the record field structure**
o   **Make a backup copy**

Data Base Management

A DBMS or data base management system such as dBASE III PLUS allows
you to add, delete, change, sort, search for and calculate
particular information from a database using a DBMS. Your college
or university may use a DBMS to store information about you and
your courses on a computer. The information in a database is stored
in database files, much like it would be stored in file folders.
The files are stored on disks, much like file folders are stored
in filing cabinets. dBASE III PLUS allows you to enter and use the
information in your database file just like you would with data in
file folders, except that the computer quickly performs searches,
sorts, calculations, and reports. The examples presented in this
tutorial are just illustrations. They could, however, be used by
many small businesses in their day-to-day operations.

There are a number of uses or applications for dBASE III PLUS
including:
    Mailing lists (membership and subscription lists)
    Accounting (bookkeeping and accounting information)
    Scientific Research (experimental data, scientific journals)
    Business information (customers, vendors, inventories)
    Personal use (home records, book library)
    Library and Government databases (scientific, academic and
       agency publications)

9

As the DOS Tutorial pointed out to you, it is possible to use an application effectively without knowing much about DOS! It is also just as possible for you to use dBASE III PLUS without knowing its full capabilities and possibilities. You will learn how to use the ASSIST mode menu system for dBASE III PLUS.

Help Facility

Whenever you encounter difficulties, have a question, or want to learn more, the dBASE help facility is ready to offer assistance. Help is available from a file within dBASE III PLUS itself.

In the ASSIST mode, position the selection bar on the appropriate command and press [F1]. Each command has a short explanation in the help file. To return to the ASSIST mode, strike any key. You can only position the selection bar on those menu items that are possible to execute with your current file.

A second method of obtaining help is to use the DOT prompt mode. The DOT prompt mode is a useful method of learning about any data base command at any time.

To branch to the DOT prompt mode, press **[Esc]**, type **HELP**, and press **[Enter]**. The command will be executed and you will see a MAIN MENU as shown in Figure 1-1. You can select any of the menu choices and sub-menus to further explore the workings of dBASE III PLUS.

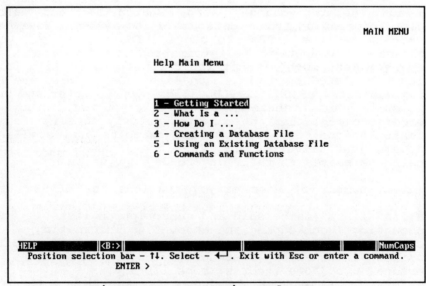

Figure 1-1:   Main Help Menu

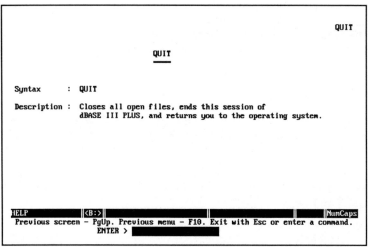

```
                                                              QUIT


                        QUIT
                        ──

      Syntax      :  QUIT

      Description :  Closes all open files, ends this session of
                     dBASE III PLUS, and returns you to the operating system.
```

```
HELP            <B:>                                      NumCaps
Previous screen - PgUp. Previous menu - F10. Exit with Esc or enter a command.
                    ENTER >
```

Figure 1-2:   Help Screen for QUIT Command

In the advance stage of obtaining help, you can type HELP followed by the name of the command or function that you would like to use. For example, type **HELP QUIT   [Enter]**, and you would see on the screen Figure 1-2. If you have a color monitor and graphics card, you can temporarily change the screen from black and white to color, or if you have a monochrome screen, you can change the intensity of the screen and cause blinking. Use the Help facility for the command of SET COLOR.

To access the options shown below the status line, press the key indicated. To return to the ASSIST mode at any time, press **[F2]**.

Setting the Default Drive and Path

You are using a work disk in drive A, so you need to set the default drive and path. The default drive is the disk drive where dBASE III PLUS expects to find your data files. You will need to set the default drive each time you enter dBASE III PLUS. The default drive and path can be changed in the ASSIST mode by using the appropriate menus.

> Type **T** to move to the **Tools** option.
> Select the first option on the menu, **Set drive:**

Press **[Enter]**
> The Set drive options screen appears. This Tools utility has many uses. One use is to change the default drive and directory. To change the default drive to "A," highlight the letter "**A**" in the menu.

Press **[Enter]**
> This changes the default drive and directory. Note that the completion of a menu procedure always returns you to the pulldown menu of the command options.

Creating a Database File in the ASSIST Mode

You should have the [CapsLock] key on. The word "Caps" will show on the control line at the lower right of the screen. You will also know if the "CAPS" are turned on when you begin typing.

To create the file MASTER, press **C** to select the **Create** menu and position the selection bar on **Database file** as shown in Figure 1-3, and press **[Enter]**.

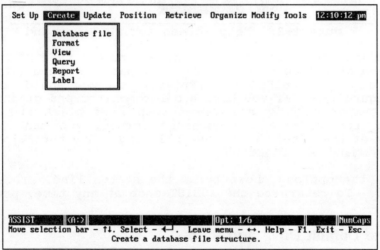

Figure 1-3: Create a Database File in ASSIST

Position the selection bar on **A:** to select drive A and press **[Enter]**. You will be asked to "Enter the name of the file:." Type **MASTER** and press **[Enter]**. NOTE: File names are from 1 to 8 letters, digits, or the underline. Names must start with a letter. The system automatically adds a three character extension ".DBF" to indicate the type of file.

The system will display Figure 1-4 on the screen which allows you to assign field names and describe the format of the data to be stored in each field of the record in the MASTER file.

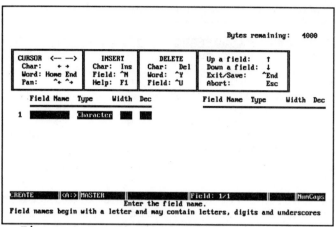

Figure 1-4: Start of Master File Record
Structure

Before typing in the data contained in Table 1-1, the following
information will help you understand what each of the components
of a field in a record represents:

FIELD NAME   The field name selected is usually one which
                   represents the contents. The maximum length
                   of a field name is 10 characters. The field
                   name must start with a letter and can contain
                   additional letters, digits, and underscore.
                   The field name cannot contain spaces.

TYPE   This component indicates whether the field
                   contents are alphabetic (C), numeric (N), a
                   date (D), logical (L), or a memo (M). The
                   field type can be changed by typing the first
                   letter of the TYPE or pressing the space bar
                   until the correct type appears and then press
                   [Enter].

WIDTH   The number of spaces which you want to set
                   aside for the field contents is specified in
                   numeric terms. An alphabetic field is from
                   1 - 254 characters, numeric is 1 - 19 digits
                   (including sign and decimal point), date is
                   automatically 8, logical is automatically 1,
                   and memo is of varying length.

DEC   DEC is the abbreviation for identifying the
                   number of decimal places (0 - 15) which you
                   want in a numeric type field. The number of
                   decimal places must be at least 2 places less
                   than specified in the width specification.

13

Table 1-1:   MASTER File Record Format

FIELD NUMBER	FIELD NAME	TYPE	WIDTH	DEC
1	ACCT_NUM	N	6	0
2	CUST_NAME	C	20	
3	STREET	C	20	
4	CITY_STATE	C	20	
5	ZIP	C	5	
6	BEGIN_BAL	N	10	2
7	UPDAT_BAL	N	10	2
8	CR_LIMIT	N	10	2

Table 1-1 shows a file record with eight fields of information. To enter the first field in the record whose name is ACCT_NUM,

> Type **ACCT_NUM [Enter]**

To change the type of field from character to numeric,

> Type **N**

To enter the field width,

> Type **6 [Enter]**

And finally, enter the number of decimal places,

> Type **0 [Enter]**

This will complete the information to enter the first field into the database file.   Continue typing in the next field name for field number 2: **CUST_NAME [Enter] [Enter] 20 [Enter]**.   This will place you at field number 3. Type in the remaining lines from Table 1-1, starting with STREET and ending with field number 8.

After creating the final field (CR_LIMIT) in the record, press **[Enter]** once for the blank field and then a second time to confirm the end of the operation. When the system displays the question, "Input data records now? (Y/N)," respond by typing in **N**. You will be returned to the dBASE III PLUS ASSIST menu mode.

You have now created a file called MASTER, defined the number of fields in a record, the field names, type of field, and the length of the field.

Display Record Field Structure

To display your record field structure on the screen, press **T** for **Tools**, and position the selection bar on **List structure** and press **[Enter]**. When the prompt of, "Direct the output to the printer? [Y/N]" appears, type **Y** if you want both screen display and printed output. Otherwise, type **N** for screen display.

Press any key to return to the ASSIST menu.

Add New Records - Append

Before you can enter additional data into the database file, you must have the proper file stored in the computer primary memory. With the MASTER database file in the computer memory, press **U** to select the **Update** menu. Position the selection bar on the **Append** option and press **[Enter]**.

You can begin adding data into your database by entering the appropriate information for each field in the first record, and continuing to do so for subsequent records. If you make an error entering your data, do not be concerned. You will learn how to correct the entries. You will add the five records shown in Table 1-2 and save them. The account number for the first record is 2145.

> Type **2145 [Enter]**
> The cursor moves to the next field. The customer name is MURPHY.

> Type **MURPHY [Enter]**

> The cursor moves to the third field.

Table 1-2: Data Values for MASTER File Records

Field Name	Rec 1	Rec 2	Rec 3	Rec 4	Rec 5
ACCT_NUM	2145	4115	4155	6598	6155
CUST_NAME	MURPHY	ADAMS	JONES	MCCLURE	ODEGARD
STREET	23 OAK	412 ELY	345 ELM	986 OAK	98 ELM
CITY_STATE	LEE, IL	MAR, CA	LEE, IL	LEE, IL	OAK, CA
ZIP	78374	95485	78374	78374	96254
BEGIN_BAL	150.00	200.00	300.00	300.00	100.00
UPDAT_BAL	150.00	600.00	300.00	500.00	400.00
CR_LIMIT	4000.00	3000.00	2000.00	1000.00	2500.00

> Finish entering data for the first record.
> When your data completely fills the field width, like the zip code, the computer beeps and the cursor automatically jumps to the next field. When you are

entering data, you can use the cursor movement keys to correct data already entered. When you have entered data for the last field in the record, a new, blank, record appears for you to enter data in the next record.

Complete the entering of data for the remaining records.

When you have finished entering the data from Table 1-2 and before pressing [Enter] for $2500.00 in record 5:

Press **[Ctrl]-[End]**
You have saved the records and returned to the ASSIST menu mode.

List the Data Entries

To display your database entries on the screen, press **R** for **Retrieve**, position the selection bar on **List**, and press **[Enter]**. Press **[Enter]** when the next submenu appears with the prompt of "Execute the command" highlighted. When the next prompt of, "Direct the output to the printer? [Y/N]" appears, type **N**. If you type Y, the same information that appears on the screen will be printed.

Quick Review

You have just learned how to create a file and how to enter data into a database file using the ASSIST mode menus. You saved the five records by pressing [Ctrl]-[End] and returned to the ASSIST mode menu. You next chose the List option from the Retrieve menu to display the data entries on the screen or the printer.

Creating a Database File from the DOT Prompt

You can create database files from the DOT prompt instead of from the ASSIST mode. For this you need to learn specific commands. As a practice exercise, you will create a transaction file for accounts receivable. Again, you need to design the structure first. Table 1-3 shows the structure for ARTRAN, the accounts receivable transaction file. It contains seven fields. Note that the sixth field is a date field. Date fields are eight characters by default with a format of month/day/year.

To exit to the DOT prompt:

Press **[Esc]**
You are now ready to create the database file. CREATE is
the DOT prompt command which is used to create a database
file, followed by the file name.

Type **CREATE ARTRAN [Enter]**
The Database utility appears. You used the Database
utility earlier to enter the structure for MASTER. This
time, you will enter the structure for ARTRAN. Using the
information from Table 1-3:

Enter the information for the seven fields.

Table 1-3: ARTRAN Transaction File Format

FIELD NUMBER	FIELD NAME	TYPE	WIDTH	DECIMAL PLACES
1	ACCT_NUM	N	6	0
2	REF_NO	N	6	0
3	TRAN_CD	N	1	0
4	PROD_CD	N	2	0
5	AGE_CD	N	1	0
6	DATE	D	8	
7	AMOUNT	N	10	2

After you have completed entering the seventh field:

Press **[Enter]**
You will see a message on the screen, asking you to
confirm the end of the operation.

Press **[Enter]**
The screen displays the question, "Input data records
now? (Y/N)."

Press **Y.**
You will now be able to type the data for each field.

Enter data for the four records.

After entering the data for these four records and before pressing
[Enter] for $10.00 in record 4, press [Ctrl]-[End] to save the
entries and return to the DOT prompt.

Table 1-4: Data Records for ARTRAN File

Field	Rec 1	Rec 2	Rec 3	Rec 4
1	6598	6155	2145	4155
2	11458	11459	77145	77146
3	4	4	1	1
4	0	0	45	39
5	1	1	0	0
6	011788	011788	011788	011788
7	-75.00	-13.50	50.00	10.00

Press **[Ctrl]-[End]**
> You will automatically be returned to the DOT prompt.
> To view data on the screen using the DOT prompt, use the
> LIST command [F3].

Type **LIST [Enter]** or press **[F3]**
> The screen displays the data you entered into the
> currently open file, which is ARTRAN. If you see some
> errors, do not try to correct them now. You will learn
> how to edit data later.

Making a Backup Copy of Your Database

In business, the accounts receivable master file is very important:
It indicates how much money customers owe the company. If it were
to become lost or seriously damaged, the company could suffer
devastating consequences. Therefore, many businesses maintain a
rigorous backup policy with regard to crucial computer files. You
can copy a disk file in dBASE III PLUS from the DOT prompt.

Use the following DOT prompt steps to copy the file, ARTRAN, to a
backup file, ARTRANBU, on the same disk. To copy the current open
database file to a file of another name,

Type **COPY TO ARTRANBU [Enter]**
> A message appears, indicating that 4 records were copied.

You can check that the copy procedure worked. To check the copy:

Type **DIR [Enter]** or press **[F4]**
> You should see that both ARTRAN.DBF and ARTRANBU.DBF are
> listed. They will not have the same size until ARTRAN
> has been saved to disk.

You have created a backup copy of ARTRAN in case any damage occurs. This copy will also be useful when you modify your original database in later lessons. That is, you will still have a copy of your original database. From time to time in the tutorial, you will use the backup copy of the database.

It is a good idea to back up your database files regularly. If the information is important, like an accounts receivable file, you should make more than one copy and store at least one copy on a different disk in a different location from your computer and original data. (If you have two floppy disk drives, the command COPY TO B:ARTRANBU copies the file to a disk in drive B.) This will ensure the safety of your database files and prevent the loss of valuable time and data.

Saving a file

You save a file to disk by closing it. The best method for closing files from the DOT prompt is to use the command CLOSE ALL. This command closes all the files that are currently open.

>   Type **CLOSE ALL   [Enter]**
>   There is now no active database in memory.

Quick Review

You created a file, ARTRAN, from the DOT prompt and entered the data for the records. You also saved directly to disk a backup "copy" of the current file in RAM. To save the current file to disk, you closed the file.

You can continue or quit once you have completed this last operation. However, failure to close the files before turning the computer off can result in lost of data!

Summary

You have learned how to create a database file in both the ASSIST mode and the DOT prompt. Also you know how to display its structure on the screen and have it printed. In addition to making a backup copy of the file, you used the command CLOSE ALL to save the file on disk.

REVIEW QUESTION

1.   How is a file created in dBASE III PLUS:
     a.   In the ASSIST mode?

b.   In the DOT prompt mode?

2.   How is data entered into a database file once the file is created?

3.   How do you save your new database file on your student disk (as opposed to saving it in the computer RAM memory)?

4.   How do you make a backup copy of a file? Describe the steps.

Table 1-5:   Cursor Navigation Keys

Key	Movement or Action	Work Surface
→	Right one position	
←	Left one position	
↓	Down one row	
	Next field	Edit
↑	Up one row	
	Previous field	Edit
[PgDn]	Display next screen	Browse, Edit, word wrap
	Bottom of pulldown menu	ASSIST
[PgUp]	Display previous screen	Browse, Edit, word wrap
	Top of pulldown menu	ASSIST
[End]	End of field	Edit
	Last field in record	Browse
	Last text/field on line	Word wrap
	Next column within field	Modify
[Home]	Beginning of field	Edit
	Beginning of record	Browse
	Indent (or left margin)	Word wrap
	Beginning of previous field	Modify
[Backspace]	Delete previous character	
[Ctrl]-[Bkspace]	Delete previous word	Word wrap
[Tab]	Next field	Edit, Browse
	Next tab stop	Word wrap (if insert is off)
	Next column	Lists, tables

LESSON 2

Retrieving a File
and Modifying the
Record Contents and Structure

After completing this lesson, you will be able to:
o   Retrieve a file
o   Add a new field to an existing record structure
o   Modify a field in an existing record structure
o   List a record field structure
o   Branch to a specific record
o   Edit the contents of a record

Modify Command

The options within the submenu of the Modify command can be used
to change a number of different structures of the database,
including the database file itself. In this exercise, you are to
change the configuration of the fields within the file's records.

Retrieve a File Using the ASSIST Mode

1.   If the database file is not currently in memory, move to the
      Set Up command in the main menu, position the selection bar
      on the **Database file** option, and press **[Enter]**.

2.   Select drive **A** and press **[Enter]**.

3.   Select **MASTER.DBF** and press **[Enter]**.
          Type N to the prompt of "Is the file indexed [Y/N]."

4.   Press **N**
          The file has been retrieved and is now available for use.

Add a field - Memo

You will now modify the structure of the MASTER record to include
a memo field. A memo field is an entry of text material of up to
5,000 characters. dBASE III PLUS automatically makes the field

length 10 characters and stores the information in a separate file on the disk.

To enter text data to memo field, do the following:
1. Press **M** for **Modify**, then position the selection bar on **Database file** and press **[Enter]**.

2. Move the cursor to field 9.

3. Type name of field, **TEXT**, and press **[Enter]**.

4. Type **M** for memo

5. Press **[Ctrl]-[End]** to save the modification.

6. Press **[Enter]** to confirm the modification.

You will be returned to the main menu after step 6.

Modify the File Record Structure

You will find at times that the initial file structure design will be unsatisfactory as you work with the database. Through the use of the Modify command and the File Structure option, you can adjust the fields of all of the records. It is easier to modify an old file even if it contains considerable data in it.

Change the CITY_STATE field width to 15 characters and the ZIP field width to 9 characters. The MASTER file must be in current memory.

1. Press **M** for **Modify**, position selection bar on **Database file**, and press **[Enter]**.

2. Position cursor on CITY_STATE field width column, type **15**, and press **[Enter]**.

3. Position cursor on ZIP field width column, type **9**, and press **[Enter]**.

4. Press **[Ctrl]-[End]** to indicate end of file structure changes.

5. Press **[Enter]** to confirm changes.

All records in the database will be changed to the new file structure before control returns to the main menu.

To check on the changes you have made to the file structure, press **T** for **Tools**, position the selection bar to **List structure**, and press **[Enter]**. When the prompt of "Direct the output to the printer? [Y/N]" is displayed, type **N** to show the record structure on the screen only.

The record structure will be displayed on the screen along with information about which file it represents, number of records in the database, and date of last change to any part of the file.

Striking any key will return control for you to the main menu.

Goto Record

The Position command in the main menu has an option called Goto Record. This option allows you the user to specifically position the internal pointer to a particular record. Within the submenu, you can choose to place the pointer at the TOP of the file, or the BOTTOM of the file, or any record in between by using the Goto Record. If you choose the Goto Record, the prompt will want to know the specific record number at which to place the pointer.

A reason that you might want to use the Goto Record option is to modify a certain record in the file because some facet of it may have changed like the contents of the address field.

Edit - Change Record Contents

The Edit option is used to change the contents of any or all parts of a record as well as any or all of the records. When you invoke the Edit option, the internal pointer identifying a particular record remains unchanged from the previous operation.

If the internal pointer is not at the right record to be modified, it can be changed by either of two methods. One is the use of the Goto Record option within the Position command. The Goto Record option is preferable if the desired record is many (15 or more) records away from the present pointer location. The second method is to invoke the Edit option and then use the [PgUp] or the [PgDn] keys to position the pointer.

Since you have new material to add to the record as shown in Table 2-1, you can begin with record one in the file by utilizing the Goto Record option in the Position command. The following steps will enable you to start with record number one in the file:

1. Press **P** to move to the **Position** command in the main menu.

2. Position the selection bar on the **Goto Record** option and press **[Enter]**.

3.   Position the selection bar in the new submenu on the **TOP** option for record number 1 in the file and press **[Enter]**.

4.   Move to the **Update** command in the main menu.

5.   Position the selection bar on the **Edit** option and press **[Enter]**.

6.   Move the cursor to field number nine, TEXT.

7.   Press **[Ctrl]-[Home]** to enter memo text.   Enter the text material. For record one, type: **Always pays promptly.**

8.   Press **[Ctrl]-[W]** to save the text you have just entered.

9.   Press **[PgDn]** to move to the next record. Repeat steps 6-9 as many times as necessary to complete all the entries as displayed in Table 2-1.

10. After all entries have been completed, press **[Ctrl]-[End]** to save the records and return to the main menu.

Table 2-1:   Comments for Memo Field

Record Number	Memo comments
1	Always pays promptly
2	Credit is excellent. Never uses full credit limit.
3	Credit is good. Slow but steady pay off.
4	Active credit user. Always charges with card, but slow to pay.
5	BAD CREDIT RISK! Follow up!

Summary

You have just learned a number of important features of dBASE III PLUS: how to modify a file's structure; and how to position the file pointer.

Retrieve

The Retrieve command in the main menu is utilized to display and print records from the current database and to create report forms and labels. It is also used to perform a limited amount of statistical work in the form of computing sums, averages and the counting of records in a database. Table 2-2 shows the type of actions which each of the options accomplishes.

Table 2-2:   Retrieve Command Options

Option	Purpose
List	Used to display on the screen or print specific records and fields from the current database. Use the Display option if you want to have the listing pause periodically.
Display	Same as the List option except it will pause if the list is greater than the screen's capacity.
Report	Used to produce the actual report initially created in the Create command option. Specific conditions can be imposed to display selected records.
Label	Used to print the actual label created in the Create command option. Limiting conditions can be imposed to print only selected records from the current database.
Sum	Used to compute the total of selected fields in the current database.
Average	Used to compute the mean numeric value of selected fields in the current database.
Count	Used to compute the number of records in the current database which meet a specified condition.

List Records Using the ASSIST Mode

The List option in the Retrieve command is a quick way to see the results of any action performed on the database. It can be as simple as listing of the contents of all the fields for each record in the file or it can be a listing of only those records within the database which meet certain conditions.

Using the List option, you can see on the screen or have printed the customer names which have a particular ZIP code, or those with a balance of more than $2,000, or those who are college graduates and under 35 years of age.

List - All Records

In the simplest mode, the following steps will display on the screen all of the records and their fields in a database:

1. Type **R** for the **Retrieve** command in the main menu, position the selection bar on the **List** option, and press **[Enter]**.

2. Position the selection bar on the **Execute the command** option and press **[Enter]**.

3. Type **N** in response to the prompt of "Direct the output to the printer? [Y/N]."

Every field of every record in the database will now be shown on the screen. Use the List option to display on the screen or print the results of either the replacement of text or the results of an arithmetic operation.

List - Specific Fields

In the following example, you are to list only the fields of: CUST_NAME; CITY_STATE; ZIP; and UPDAT_BAL.

1. Type **R** for the **Retrieve** command in the main menu, position the selection bar on the **List** option, and press **[Enter]**.

2. Position the selection bar on the **Construct a field list** option and press **[Enter]**.

3. Position the selection bar on the **CUST_NAME** field and press **[Enter]**. Repeat the step 3 process for each of the following fields: CITY-STATE; ZIP; and UPDAT_BAL.

4. Press either the [→] or [←] key to move to the next submenu. Position the selection bar on the **Execute the command** and press **[Enter]**.

5. Type **N** in response to the prompt of "Direct the output to the printer? [Y/N]."

Again, all of the records of the database are listed but this time with a reduced number of fields.

List - Specific Records

In the next example you are to list only those records that have the UPDAT_BAL of less than $300. In addition, you are to list the CUST_NAME field as well as the UPDAT_BAL field of those meeting the 'less than' $300 parameter.

1. Type **R** for the **Retrieve** command in the main menu, position the selection bar on the **List** option, and press **[Enter]**.

2. Position the selection bar on the **Construct a field list** option and press **[Enter]**.

3. Position the selection bar on the **CUST_NAME** field and press **[Enter]**. Repeat the process for the UPDAT_BAL field.

4. Press either the [→] or [←] key to move to the next submenu. Position the selection bar on the **Specify scope** option and press **[Enter]**.

5. Select the **Default scope** option which in this case is the same as ALL and press **[Enter]**.

6. Position the selection bar on the **Build a search condition** option and press **[Enter]**.

7. Select the **UPDAT_BAL** field and press **[Enter]**.

8. Position the selection bar on the **Less than** option and press **[Enter]**.

9. Type **300** in response to the prompt and then press **[Enter]**.

10. Press **[Enter]** to confirm that there are **No more conditions**.

11. Position the selection bar on the **Execute the command** option and press **[Enter]**.

12. Type **N** in response to the prompt of "Direct the output to the printer? [Y/N]."

As before, all of the records of the database that meet the criteria of an Updated balance of less than $300 are listed on the screen.

This concludes the exercise using the ASSIST mode. Before closing the file, make a backup copy of MASTER using the procedure as outlined in Lesson 1.

Quick Review

In the list option of the Retrieve command, you learned to list all fields of all records and also how to list certain fields of all records. Additionally, you also learned to list only those records meeting certain conditions. The List option is a powerful tool enabling you to check on actions which you executed in a previous operation.

Retrieving a File Using the DOT Prompt

To retrieve and open a file, the USE command is typed followed by the file name. The USE command closes the current (if any) file in RAM and brings into memory the specific file named.

> Type **USE ARTRAN [Enter]**
> The file name appears on the status line at the bottom of the screen. Presently, it contains four (4) records.

Displaying Data from the DOT Prompt

After retrieving a file, you can enter commands from the DOT prompt to display the file record structure and the data in the file's records. You will practice using some display commands from the DOT prompt.

Display Record Field Structure

In the ASSIST mode, you listed the file structure by making menu selections. From the DOT prompt, you will print by issuing a command. The DISPLAY STRUCTURE command displays the file structure on the screen, and the LIST STRUCTURE TO PRINT command prints out the file structure. At the DOT prompt:

> Type **DISPLAY STRUCTURE [Enter]** or press **[F5]**
> The structure of the record will be displayed on your screen. Next, in order to print the data structure:

> Type **LIST STRUCTURE TO PRINT [Enter]**
> A copy of the file structure will be printed.

Positioning the Record Pointer

LIST and DISPLAY, each without any parameters (such as ALL), perform differently. LIST displays all records, while DISPLAY shows only the current record.

> Type **LIST [Enter]** or press **[F3]**
> All the records in the file are displayed.

> Type **DISPLAY [Enter]** or press **[F8]**
> Nothing is displayed.

The current record, shown on the status bar, is EOF, or End Of File. You must reset the record pointer. Rec EOF/4 on the status line at the bottom of the screen alerts you to the fact that you are at the end of the file. Always check to be sure you are at the beginning of a file when displaying data. To get to the beginning of the file:

Type **GOTO RECORD 1 [Enter]**
You have reset the record pointer to the first record. You could also have entered the command as GOTO TOP. You may want to enter the command HELP GOTO to see the options which are used with the GOTO command.

Displaying All Records

Type **USE MASTER [Enter]**
When one database file is in use and you give the command to use another, the first database is automatically closed. The easiest way to see the data is to use the DISPLAY command.

Type **DISPLAY [Enter]** or press **[F8]**
The screen shows the data for all fields of the current record (the first record), including the record number.

Type **DISPLAY ALL [Enter]**
As shown in Figure 2-1, the screen shows all records in the file. Each record is displayed on two lines. When the file contains more records than can be displayed on the screen, the display pauses when the screen is full and prompts you to press any key to continue.

```
. DISPLAY
Record#  ACCT_NUM CUST_NAME         STREET              CITY_STATE   ZIP
         BEGIN_BAL UPDAT_BAL  CR_LIMIT TEXT
      1     2145 MURPHY               23 OAK              LEE, IL      7837
4        150.00    157.50  4000.00 Memo

. DISPLAY ALL
Record#  ACCT_NUM CUST_NAME         STREET              CITY_STATE   ZIP
         BEGIN_BAL UPDAT_BAL  CR_LIMIT TEXT
      1     2145 MURPHY               23 OAK              LEE, IL      7837
4        150.00    157.50  4000.00 Memo
      2     4115 BROWN                100 ELM             MAR, CA      7837
4        200.00    630.00  3000.00 Memo
      3     4155 JONES                345 ELM             LEE, IL      7837
4        300.00    315.00  2000.00 Memo
      4     6598 MCCLURE              2150 MAIN STREET    LEE, IL      7837
4        300.00    525.00  1000.00 Memo
      5     6155 ODEGARD              2150 MAIN STREET    OAK, CA      9625
4        100.00    420.00  2500.00 Memo
.
Command Line  <A:> MASTER                         Rec: EOF/5            NumCaps
              Enter a dBASE III PLUS command.
```

Figure 2-1: Displaying All Records

29

You do not really need to see the record numbers. To turn off the display of record numbers:

Type **LIST OFF [Enter]**

The DISPLAY and LIST commands are very similar. LIST does not pause when the screen is full (you can press [Ctrl]-[S] at any time to pause the screen during LIST), so it is more suitable for printing data. If you use the pause, press either [Space] or [Enter] to continue the listing. The OFF parameter causes the display to omit record numbers. The DOT prompt commands of LIST and DISPLAY ALL, when invoked, do not care where the record pointer is located. The DISPLAY command does.

The LIST command is also used to print data. The command to print data is LIST TO PRINTER. However, you will not print the data at this time.

Displaying Selected Fields

If you do not want to display all the fields in the file, you can specify only those fields to be displayed using the DISPLAY or LIST command. Suppose you just want to see the data for three specific fields in record one of the file.

Type **GOTO RECORD 1 [Enter]**

Type **DISPLAY CUST_NAME, UPDAT_BAL, ZIP [Enter]**
The screen displays the data for those fields in record one of the file.

Now, try this with the ARTRAN file.

Type **USE ARTRAN [Enter]**

Type **LIST ACCT_NUM, REF_NO, AMOUNT [Enter]**
The data for those three fields is displayed for all the records in the file.

Displaying Selected Records

You can select the records you want displayed, rather than displaying all the records in the file. You do this by specifying the condition that has to be met for a record to be displayed. The condition follows the command word FOR. For example, you might want to display only those records with the AMOUNT less than zero (negative).

Type **DISPLAY FOR AMOUNT <0 ACCT_NUM, AMOUNT [Enter]**

30

To select records based on a numeric field, the arithmetic relation that must be met is specified in the LIST or DISPLAY command. You can try another example.

Type **USE MASTER [Enter]**

Type **DISPLAY FOR UPDAT_BAL>300 CUST_NAME, UPDAT_BAL [Enter]**
The expression you gave for selecting records is for the UPDAT_BAL to be more than $300. Records that did not meet that criterion were not displayed.

To locate and display selected records based on the contents of character fields, the character field contents must match exactly the characters between either double or single quotes in the DOT command. As an example,

Type **DISPLAY FOR CITY_STATE='LEE, IL' CUST_NAME, CITY_STATE [Enter]**
This displays records with a city and state of LEE, IL. The screen displays only those records where the contents of the character field matches exactly what you have placed between the quotes, including the comma and the case of the letters. (Figure 2-2) It is important that you type in the contents of the field in the same case as used in the file. That is, "LEE, IL" is not considered equal to "Lee, IL," because the latter contains lowercase letters.

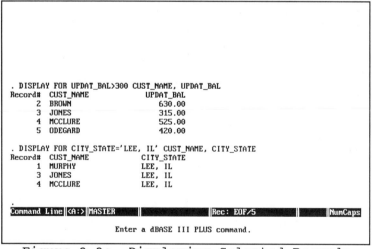

```
. DISPLAY FOR UPDAT_BAL>300 CUST_NAME, UPDAT_BAL
Record#  CUST_NAME            UPDAT_BAL
     2   BROWN                   630.00
     3   JONES                   315.00
     4   MCCLURE                 525.00
     5   ODEGARD                 420.00

. DISPLAY FOR CITY_STATE='LEE, IL' CUST_NAME, CITY_STATE
Record#  CUST_NAME            CITY_STATE
     1   MURPHY               LEE, IL
     3   JONES                LEE, IL
     4   MCCLURE              LEE, IL
.
```
Command Line ‖<A:>‖MASTER ‖   ‖Rec: EOF/5 ‖   ‖NumCaps‖
Enter a dBASE III PLUS command.

Figure 2-2: Displaying Selected Records

Whenever you want to locate any record which might contain a specific sequence of characters, use the $ operator in place of the = operator in such a situation. For example,

31

Type **LIST FOR 'CA' $ CITY_STATE [Enter]**
You could read the command as "List for 'CA' contained in CITY_STATE." If you had an entry of ITHACA, NY in CITY_STATE, that record would also match the criterion specified in the above command because ITHACA contains a CA.

You can continue or quit once you have completed this last operation of the lesson. If you decide to quit, remember to CLOSE ALL open files because failure to close the files before turning the computer off can result in lost of data!

Summary

You have learned to List and Display all of the records, some of the fields of all of the records, and some of the records in a file. Also you have learned how to position the internal file pointer in both the ASSIST and the DOT modes to facilitate either the listing or displaying of a record or records.

REVIEW QUESTIONS

1. How do you retrieve a file using the:
    a) ASSIST mode?
    b) DOT prompt?

2. How do you modify a file's structure to add a field, and change the field length?

3. How do you position the file pointer to a particular record?

4. How do you change the existing contents of a field?

5. What does the [Ctrl]-[End] key combination do when you are editing a record?

6. What is the result of the DISPLAY command?

7. What is the purpose of the $ in the LIST FOR command?

8. What is the smallest part of a record that can be displayed?

LESSON 3
Replacing
and
Listing Records

After completing this lesson, you will be able to:
o   Do global record replacement
o   List specific fields of records
o   List specific records

Changing Contents Directly

The Update command in the main menu is a very versatile command.
Table 3-1 illustrates the actions which you can achieve through the
use of the Update command.   In this exercise you will use the
Replace option.

Table 3-1:   Update Command Options

Option	Purpose
Append	Used to add new records to the current file beginning at the end of the file.
Edit	Used to change the field contents of existing records.
Display	Used to display from 1 to 15 records at a time on the screen.
Browse	Used to display, edit, and append records in the current file.
Replace	Used to replace the field contents in one or more records.
Delete	Used to identify records to be purged from the file when the Pack option is executed.

Recall	Used to unmark records previously marked in the Delete option.
Pack	Used to remove records from the database marked by the Delete option.

Replace Records Using the ASSIST Mode

You can change the contents of a field in all or some of the records in the file through the use of the Replace option. In the following example you want to change all of the records that have a misspelling of a city name in the MASTER file. You need to change the name of LEE, IL to LEI, IL in the CITY_STATE field. After retrieving the MASTER file, the following steps illustrate how quickly and painlessly you can make the changes:

1. Type **U** for **Update** in the main menu, position the selection bar on the **Replace** option, and press **[Enter]**.

2. Position the selection bar on **CITY_STATE** in the submenu and press **[Enter]**.

3. Type the new name **LEI, IL** at the prompt of "Enter character string (without quotes): and press **[Enter]**.

4. Press either the [→] or [←] key to branch to the next submenu and position the selection bar on the **"Build a search condition"** option and press **[Enter]**. This option specifies the conditional limits to be used in the execution of the completed command.

5. The computer program will now return to the previous submenu to allow you to select the particular field that would have the condition it will search for. Position the selection bar on **CITY_STATE** and press **[Enter]**.

6. Position the selection bar on the **"= Equal To"** option in the new submenu and press **[Enter]**. This logical operation statement identifies for the computer the exact condition it is to find.

7. At the prompt, type the exact string of characters which are to be replaced, **"LEE, IL"** and press **[Enter]**. (Do not include the quote marks!)

8. At this next submenu, position the selection bar on the **"No more conditions"** option and press **[Enter]**.

9. Position the selection bar on the **"Execute the command"** option and press **[Enter]**.

At this point the computer will replace all spellings of LEE, IL with LEI, IL and in the lower left corner of the screen, a message will appear indicating the number of records changed.

In addition to straight replacement, numeric fields can have their contents changed through the use of the Replace command and an arithmetic operator. Consider the situation where all credit limits are to be increased ten percent.

1. Type **U** for **Update**, position the selection bar on **Replace**, and press **[Enter]**.

2. From the new submenu, position the selection bar on **CR_LIMIT** and press **[Enter]**.

3. Press **F10** to return to the submenu and position the selection bar on **CR_LIMIT** and press **[Enter]**. Type *** 1.10** and press **[Enter]** to complete the arithmetic expression of multiplying the old credit limit value by 110 percent (use decimal value) to calculate the new value of credit limit.

4. Press either the [→] or [←] key to move to the next submenu. Position the selection bar on **Specify scope** and press **[Enter]**.

5. Position the selection bar on **ALL** and press **[Enter]**.

6. Move the selection bar to **Execute the command** and press **[Enter]**.

A message will appear in the lower left corner of the screen stating how many records were replaced.

Replace Fields Using the DOT Prompt

Although the Edit screen is useful, sometimes you need to change the data in several records. For example, suppose the zip code for LEI, IL has been changed to 78327. Your database might have several records with LEI, IL physically scattered throughout it. You can use a single REPLACE command to do all the editing. Note that ZIP was designated as a character field, even though all its contents are digits. That is because it is not used for calculations. Therefore, since it is a character field, changes entered using the REPLACE command need to be enclosed in quotation marks.

Type **REPLACE ZIP WITH "78327" FOR CITY_STATE = "LEI, IL" [Enter]**
Be sure to include the quotation marks around 78327 and LEI, IL as shown. Note that "LEI,IL" (without a space after the comma) is not equal to "LEI, IL " (with a

space). Note too that uppercase and lowercase letters are not considered equal (that is, "A" does not equal "a"). A message appears on the screen:

3 records replaced.

Type **DISPLAY FOR CITY_STATE = "LEI, IL" CUST_NAME, STREET, ZIP [Enter]**
The three records with LEI, IL for CITY_STATE are displayed. All their zip codes are now 78327.

Sometimes, the contents of a field in all the records need to be updated. Again, a single command from the DOT prompt can do it. Suppose that a 5 percent fee is assessed to all accounts, and thus all updated balances need to be increased by 5 percent. That is, the new updated balance should be 1.05 times the present value. A single dBASE III command accomplishes this.

First, move to the top or beginning of the file.

Type **GOTO TOP [Enter]**

Type **REPLACE ALL UPDAT_BAL WITH UPDAT_BAL * 1.05 [Enter]**
A message appears indicating that all 5 records were replaced. You can then see the results of the 5 percent increase by displaying the data.

Type **DISPLAY ALL CUST_NAME, CITY_STATE, ZIP, UPDAT_BAL [Enter]**
Note that all the UPDAT_BAL fields have the new values (Figure 3-1).

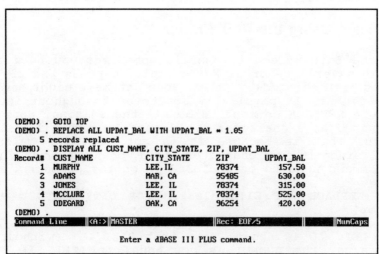

Figure 3-1:   Revised UPDAT_BAL

36

Thus, you have seen how to edit a record, using either the record number or the content of a field in the record to select the one desired. You have learned how to replace the contents of a specified field of several, or even all, records with a single command from the DOT prompt.

After making these changes, you should copy the contents of this file to another database file for backup purposes.

> Type **COPY TO MASTERBU [Enter]**
> You see the following message:

MASTERBU.dbf already exists, overwrite it? (Y/N)

The file MASTERBU already exists; you created it in a previous lesson.

> Press **Y** for Overwrite.
> The contents of MASTER.DBF are copied to MASTERBU.DBF.

Quick Review

You have learned the specifics of using the Replace command. In the Replace command you learned that you can replace all occurrences of a given condition (i.e. a misspelled word). You also learned that you can compute values for numeric fields. In addition, you also learned how to use the REPLACE command to change data in several or all the records with a single command.

The SUM, COUNT, and AVERAGE Functions

There are several useful functions within dBASE III PLUS that are available from the DOT prompt. SUM, COUNT, and AVERAGE are three functions that are easy to use.

> Type **SUM UPDAT_BAL [Enter]**

> Type **SUM UPDAT_BAL FOR CITY_STATE='LEI, IL' [Enter]**

> Type **AVERAGE UPDAT_BAL FOR CITY_STATE='LEI, IL' [Enter]**

> Type **COUNT FOR CITY_STATE='LEI, IL' [Enter]**
> Your screen should look like Figure 3-2. If there is a misspelling or a mismatch when selecting records based on character field criteria, then the message "No records" appears.

```
(DEMO) . SUM UPDAT_BAL
        5 records summed
     UPDAT_BAL
        2047.50
(DEMO) . SUM UPDAT_BAL FOR CITY_STATE = 'LEI, IL'
        3 records summed
     UPDAT_BAL
         997.50
(DEMO) . AVERAGE UPDAT_BAL FOR CITY_STATE='LEI, IL'
        3 records averaged
  UPDAT_BAL
      332.50
(DEMO) . COUNT FOR CITY_STATE='LEI, IL'
        3 records
(DEMO) .
```

Command Line	<A:>	MASTER		Rec: EOF/5			NumCaps

Enter a dBASE III PLUS command.

Figure 3-2: Statistical Functions

Arithmetic in the DOT Prompt

The arithmetic functions of addition (+), subtraction (-), multiplication (*), division (/), and exponentiation (^) can be executed whenever the DOT prompt is shown. Parentheses can be used to change the normal sequence of arithmetic calculations. Another mathematical function which is available is the one of square root. It is written as SQRT(<arithmetic expression>).

To form the equation for the computer, enter a question mark followed by the formula. After the answer has been displayed on the screen, the DOT prompt reappears and the next equation or command can be entered.

    Type **?100.00 + 350.62** **[Enter]** (ans: 450.62)

    Type **?4321/10+10** **[Enter]** (ans: 442.10)

    Type **?4321/(10+10)** **[Enter]** (ans: 216.05)

    Type **?SQRT(2 * 200 * 100 / (50 * .24))** **[Enter]** (ans: 57.74)

If a mistake is made in the typing of the equation but not noticed until the answer has been calculated, you can retrieve the equation as typed by pressing the [↑] key and the correction made. If the square root equation answer is still on the screen, press the [↑] key and move the cursor to the 200 figure and change it to 400. Then press [Enter].

DOT Prompt History

A feature of dBASE III PLUS is the storing of the DOT commands as they are executed. Any one of the 20 previously executed DOT prompt commands can be reused through the repeated use of the [↑] key until the desired command is located and the [Enter] key is pressed. Use of this feature greatly facilitates the speed of operation of the application.

If the screen becomes too cluttered, you can clean the screen by typing the CLEAR command.

Type **CLEAR** **[Enter]**

You can continue or quit once you have completed this last operation of the lesson. If you decide to quit, remember to CLOSE ALL open files because failure to close the files before turning the computer off can result in lost of data!

Summary

The specifics of using the commands to retrieve a file and modify the contents were utilized. Learning how to list or display the records in a file and more specifically how to list certain fields has added to your ability to use dBASE III PLUS. Additionally, the arithmetic functions of SUM, AVERAGE, and COUNT were utilized along with how to use the computer to solve equations. And finally, when the screen becomes too cluttered, you can use the CLEAR command to have a clean screen. One of the most useful features of the DOT prompt mode is the History function. Through the use of the [↑] key, you can retrieve and reuse without typing, a previously executed command.

REVIEW QUESTIONS

1. What happens if you misspell or change the case in a character field in SUM, AVERAGE, or COUNT commands?

2. When you want to change the same mistake within several records, what command do you use?

3. What is the first character in the DOT prompt command when you solve an equation using dBASE III PLUS?

LESSON 4

Sorting
and
Indexing Records

After completing this lesson, you will be able to:
o   **Sort on single and multiple fields**
o   **Index a file**

Sorting Files Using the ASSIST Mode

You can sort a database by field. It does not matter whether the
field is alphabetic or numeric. The files are always sorted in
ascending order. You can sort the current database and store the
results in another database file.

Sort - Single field

To sort the database, MASTER into an alphabetical order by name,
do the following steps:

1.   Type O for **Organize** on the main menu, position the selection
      bar on the **Sort** option and press **[Enter]**.

2.   Position the selection bar on the **CUST_NAME** field and press
      [Enter].

3.   Press either the [→] or [←] key to move to the next submenu.
      Position the selection bar on drive **A** and press **[Enter]**.

4.   Type the name of the file that is to contain the sorted
      records **RECSORT1** and press **[Enter]**. Press any key at the
      completion of the sorting action to return to the main menu.

5.   To examine the file that contains the sorted records, type **S**
      for Setup, press **[Enter]**, position the selection bar on drive
      A, and press **[Enter]**.

6. Position the selection bar on the file name **RECSORT1** and press **[Enter]**. Type **N** at the prompt of "Is the file Indexed?"

7. Type **R** for Retrieve in the main menu, position the selection bar on **List**, and press **[Enter]**.

8. Position the selection bar to the **Execute the command** option and press **[Enter]**.

9. Type **N** at the prompt for sending the output to the printer. At the conclusion of the display on the screen, press any key to return to the main menu.

Sort - Multiple Fields

The act of sorting can be performed on more than one field at a time. For example, you can have the file sorted by CUST_NAME within the same ZIP code. Using the MASTER file:

1. Type **O** for **Organize** on the main menu, position the selection bar on the **Sort** option and press **[Enter]**.

2. Position the selection bar on the **ZIP** field and press **[Enter]**.

3. Position the selection bar on the **CUST_NAME** field and press **[Enter]**.

4. Press either the right [→] or left [←] key to move to the next submenu. Position the selection bar on drive **A** and press **[Enter]**.

5. Type **RECSORT2** as the name of the file that is to contain the sorted records and press **[Enter]**. Press any key at the completion of the sorting action to return to the main menu.

6. To examine the file that contains the sorted records, type **S** for Setup, press **[Enter]**, position the selection bar on drive **A**, and press **[Enter]**.

7. Position the selection bar on the file name **RECSORT2** and press **[Enter]**. Type **N** at the prompt of "Is the file indexed?"

8. Type **R** for Retrieve in the main menu, position the selection bar on **List**, and press **[Enter]**.

9. Position the selection bar to the **Execute the command** option and press **[Enter]**.

10. Type **N** at the prompt for sending the output to the printer. At the conclusion of the display on the screen, press any key to return to the main menu.

Sorting Files Using the DOT Prompt

There are several ways to organize the records in your database. One way is to create a new, sorted file. You can rearrange the records in either ascending or descending order according to any field in the database. This produces a sorted database. The disadvantage is that the sorted file is static, even when you add new records. You must perform a new sort each time you add records or edit the data.

To illustrate the SORT command in dBASE III PLUS, you will sort the MASTER file on CUST_NAME. First, you display records in the file before the sort. Press [Esc] if still in the ASSIST mode.

>   Type **LIST CUST_NAME, UPDAT_BAL, ZIP [Enter]**
>   Next, sort the file by customer names.

>   Type **SORT ON CUST_NAME TO MASTER1 [Enter]**
>   A new file, MASTER1.DBF, is created with the records sorted by customer name. You can display the new file to verify the sort.

>   Type **USE MASTER1 [Enter]**

>   Type **LIST CUST_NAME, UPDAT_BAL, ZIP [Enter]**
>   This verifies that the records in MASTER1 are sorted by customer name and similar to Figure 4-1. (Could use the History feature to retrieve this command from previous use.)

For practice, sort on some other fields.

>   Type **SORT ON UPDAT_BAL TO MASTER2 [Enter]**

>   Type **SORT ON ZIP TO MASTER3 [Enter]**
>   This creates two new files sorted by UPDAT_BAL and ZIP code. You should be able to check the new files and verify that the sorts were performed.

Quick Review

Using the Sort command in the ASSIST mode, you have created a rearranging of the current file according to one or more fields of importance.   In the DOT prompt mode, you created a new file and

stored the results of rearranging of the current file according to
a specific field. The current file was not affected.

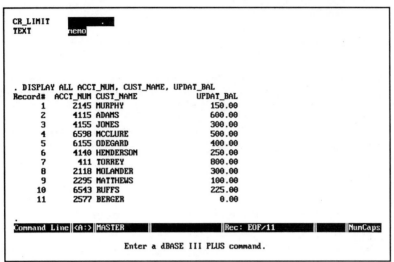

```
CR_LIMIT     █████  .
TEXT         memo




. DISPLAY ALL ACCT_NUM, CUST_NAME, UPDAT_BAL
Record#  ACCT_NUM CUST_NAME          UPDAT_BAL
      1     2145 MURPHY                 150.00
      2     4115 ADAMS                  600.00
      3     4155 JONES                  300.00
      4     6598 MCCLURE                500.00
      5     6155 ODEGARD                400.00
      6     4140 HENDERSON              250.00
      7      411 TORREY                 800.00
      8     2118 MOLANDER               300.00
      9     2295 MATTHEWS               100.00
     10     6543 RUFFS                  225.00
     11     2577 BERGER                   0.00

.
Command Line║<A:>║MASTER        ║         ║Rec: EOF/11   ║     ║NumCaps
            Enter a dBASE III PLUS command.
```

Figure 4-1:

Creating Indexes Using the DOT Mode

In contrast to the SORT command, the INDEX command creates a file
that maintains the database in logical order even when new records
are added. The advantage of indexing is the automatic updating for
records added, deleted, or edited when the index file is used with
the database. Thus, the index file makes the database file appear
to be in a specified order when it is displayed. The manipulation
is done in RAM and does not affect the physical order of the
database.

Using the MASTER file in the following example, notice that the
INDEX file is arranged alphabetically by name within zip and the
database file (MASTER) record numbers remain affected by indexing.

INDEX FILE (sequence) MASTER File Record Number		Record Number	MASTER FILE (sequence)				
JONES	3	1	MURPHY	23 OAK	LEI IL.	78327
MCCLURE	4	2	ADAMS	412 ELY	MAR CA.	95485
MURPHY	1	3	JONES	345 ELM	LEI IL.	78327
ADAMS	2	4	MCCLURE	986 ELM	LEI IL.	78327
ODEGARD	5	5	ODEGARD	98 ELM	OAK CA.	96245

You will again use MASTER. This time you will create index tags for keeping it ordered.

Type **USE MASTER [Enter]**

Type **INDEX ON CITY_STATE TO CITY_STATE [Enter]**
A message indicates that 5 records were indexed.

You created an index tag named CITY_STATE that keeps the file in alphabetical order based on the contents of the field CITY_STATE. The index tag is part of a production multiple-index file, MASTER.MDX, and is always kept current. This means that if records are added the index is automatically updated.

To verify that the file has been organized as specified:

Type **LIST ALL [Enter]**
You can see that the record numbers are no longer in order, but the CITY_STATE field contents determine the order of display.

Upon creation, the index tag is used to organize the records, and is called the master index. In subsequent use of the database, the master index is specified by typing the tag name after the word ORDER. For example, to use the MASTER file as ordered by the master index CITY_STATE, you would type: USE MASTER ORDER CITY_STATE.

To index the file on customer names, you create another index tag:

Type **INDEX ON CUST_NAME TO CUST_NAME [Enter]**
In the above example, you named the tag differently from the field it uses. That tag is now active. You can verify the results.

Type **LIST CUST_NAME, CITY_STATE [Enter]**
The file is now organized by the CUST_NAME tag. To illustrate the dynamic quality of indexing, you will add another record to the file.

Type **APPEND [Enter]** or press **[F9]**
This will add the following information as record 6 in the MASTER file.

Enter data for a new customer as follows:

Account number	3456
Name	DONOVAN
Street	987 MAGIC MILE
City	NEWPORT, OR
Zip	97123
Beginning balance	100.00
Updated balance	100.00
Credit limit	500.00

To exit APPEND and save the record after it has been entered,
    Press **[Ctrl]-[End]**
        To see where the new record is listed, use History
        feature or:

    Type **LIST CUST_NAME, CITY_STATE [Enter]**

You can continue or quit once you have completed this last
operation of the lesson. If you decide to quit, remember to CLOSE
ALL open files because failure to close the files before turning
the computer off can result in lost of data!

Summary

You have created sorted databases and index tags for keeping
database files ordered.

You may recall, during the file creation, that you repeatedly
entered N in the Index column for each field. During file creation,
you have the option of creating index tags. As you create files you
will use this feature in a later lesson.

REVIEW QUESTIONS

1. What is the difference between a sorted and an indexed file?

2. Which way of ordering is adaptable to new entries?

3. How do you specify the index tag to be the master index?

LESSON 5

Appending, Editing, and Deleting Records

After completing this lesson, you will be able to:

o **Retrieve a file with an index**
o **Use an index file to edit existing records**
o **Append new records to an old file**
o **Mark and delete a record or records in a file**
o **Delete an existing file**

Retrieving a File With an Index in the ASSIST Mode

Retrieving a file which has an index is not much different than a file which does not have an index. As was stated before, the advantage of indexing records precludes having to resort the entire file when new records are appended to the file. The procedure is as follows to retrieve the MASTER file:

1. Retrieve MASTER and type **Y** at the prompt of "Is the file indexed [Y/N]"

2. Position the highlighted cursor on **CITY_STA.NDX** and press **[Enter]**.

3. Because you have created two indexes for the MASTER file, position the highlighted cursor on the second option, **CUST_NAM.NDX** and press **[Enter]**.

4. Press [→] or [←] to move to the next menu.

Browse

The Browse option within the Update command is the most versatile option of all options. It enables you to utilize three other options at any time while you are in the Browse option. The three options are: (1) Append, (2) Edit, and (3) Delete.

46

Browse - Appending in the ASSIST Mode

You can add the additional records shown in Table 4-1 to the database MASTER by using the following steps:

1. Type **U** for Update in the main menu, position the selection bar on the **Browse** option, and press **[Enter]**.

2. Move the cursor towards the bottom of the screen until the prompt of "Add new records? (Y/N)" appears and then Type **Y**.

3. In the first field type **4140** and press **[Enter]**. The cursor will move to the next highlighted field.

4. Type **HENDERSON** and press **[Enter]**.

5. Type **605 3RD** and press **[Enter]**.

Table 4-1: Additional Records

Field Name	Rec 1	Rec 2	Rec 3
ACCT_NUM	4140	411	2118
CUST_NAME	HENDERSON	TORREY	MOLANDER
STREET	605 3RD	PO BOX 2	1620 BROADWAY
CITY_STATE	NEWARK, NJ	FIELDS, OR	SEATTLE, WA
ZIP	01954	97837	98031
BEGIN_BAL	150.00	200.00	300.00
UPDAT_BAL	0.00	0.00	300.00
CR_LIMIT	6000.00	2000.00	1000.00

6. Type **NEWARK, NJ** and press **[Enter]**.
   You need to press **[Ctrl]-[→]** three times to move to the fields at the right of the screen because the record length is greater then the width of the screen.

7. Type **01954** and press **[Enter]**.

8. Type **150.** and press **[Enter]**.

9. Type **250.** and press **[Enter]**.

10. Type **6000.** and press **[Enter]**.

11. Press **[Enter]** at the memo field.

12. Move the cursor back to the beginning of the next record by pressing **[Ctrl]-[←]** three times and pressing the **[Home]** key enough times until you are at the beginning of the new record.

Add the remaining records of Table 4-1 using steps 3 to 12.

To stop the feature of adding new records, move the cursor up one record.

To end the Browse option and save the changes, type **[Ctrl]-[End]**.

Browse - Editing in the ASSIST Mode

During the period of time that a business exists, customers will undergo changes and consequently the data in the files will have to be changed. These changes could include such things as new addresses, changes in credit limits, or name changes.

The Browse option allows you to move to any field within a record in the database and change the data. After retrieving the MASTER file, make the following changes as shown in Table 4-2:

Table 4-2: Record Updates

Customer Number	Field	New Information
6155	STREET	2150 MAIN STREET
4115	CUST_NAME	Change to BROWN

1. Type **U** for Update in the main menu, position the selection bar on the **Browse** option, and press **[Enter]**.

2. Position the highlighted bar to customer number **6155**. Using the appropriate [Home] and [End] key, move the cursor to the beginning of the **STREET** field, type **2150 MAIN STREET** and press **[Enter]**.

3. Position the highlighted bar to customer number **4115**. Move the cursor the beginning of the **CUST_NAME** field, type **BROWN**, and press **[Enter]**.

4. Press **[Ctrl]-[End]** to save the changes and exit the Browse option.

You can view the changes to the database file by executing the List option in the Retrieve command in the main menu.

Editing from the DOT Prompt

The DOT prompt in Command mode provides greater flexibility for editing in several ways. We will explore some of these ways in the next few steps.

> Exit from the ASSIST menu to the DOT prompt.
> The status bar shows that MASTER is in use. The record pointer is located at the end of the ninth record in the file.
>
> From the DOT prompt, the EDIT command is used to access the Edit screen. However, when you need to change data in a file, you often know which record you want to change. For example, if BROWN now lives at 100 ELM, you know that you want to change data in the record in which the content of the customer name field is BROWN. You can specify the record to edit from the DOT prompt. Remember that the contents of character fields must be enclosed in quotes.

> Type **EDIT FOR CUST_NAME = "BROWN" [Enter]**
> Be sure that BROWN is enclosed in quotation marks and that BROWN and the field's name itself are both in uppercase. The record for BROWN appears on the screen for editing.
>
> By specifying the record you want to edit in the EDIT command with a FOR clause, the program finds the appropriate record for you.

Use the [Enter] or [↓] key to move to the STREET field.

Change the data in the STREET field to **100 ELM**.

> Press **[Ctrl]-[End]**
> This saves the change and exits the Edit screen to the DOT prompt. To see the new contents of the record:

> Type **DISPLAY [Enter]** or press **[F8]**
> Sometimes, you may know the record number of the record you want to change. If you need to check or edit the data in record 4, you can do so from the DOT prompt.

Type **EDIT RECORD 4 [Enter]** or with the pointer at record 4, press **[F10]**
> The Edit screen appears showing the data for MCCLURE. The status line confirms that this is record 4 in the file.

With no corrections to be made to record 4, exit from the Edit screen to the DOT prompt.

Press **[Esc]**

Quick Review

You have learned how to add, edit, and delete selected records in your database file through the use of the Browse option. You positioned the cursor at the end of the file to add records to the database. All adding and editing actions were recorded and saved on your data disk when exiting the Browse option by pressing the [Ctrl]-[End] keys.

Deleting Records and Files From the DOT Prompt

There are several ways to delete records from a database file. However, before you continue the lesson, it is important to understand some of the terminology that dBASE III uses with regard to deleting records. When a record is deleted, it is considered to be "marked for deletion," but is not physically deleted from the database. Deleted records can be recalled, which means that their "marks for deletion" can be erased.

A database file that accumulates many deleted records takes up excessive file space on disk because the records marked for deletion are still actually in the file. It can be cleaned up by packing, which means that records not marked for deletion are copied to another file, the original database file is erased, the new file is renamed to the original file name, and all the indexes are rebuilt. This process may take several minutes for large database files, but the command to do this is simple.

First, however, you will back up your database file again.

Type **COPY TO MASTERBU.DBF [Enter]**

Delete - Single Record

To delete a single record, you can position the record pointer to that record and use the DELETE command. Suppose you want to delete the record for customer TORREY. You can locate the record by setting the master index to the customer name field, then seeking the name.

Type **SET INDEX TO CUST_NAME [Enter]**

Type **SEEK "TORREY" [Enter]**
    (Be sure to enter quotation marks around TORREY.) The
    record pointer is located on the appropriate record. You
    know how to display the contents of that record.

Display the contents of the current record to be sure you are at
the record for TORREY. Now you can delete the record.

Type **DELETE [Enter]**
    The message "1 record deleted" appears.

Type **DISPLAY [Enter]**
    The record is displayed again, but an asterisk appears
    after the record number, indicating that the record is
    marked for deletion (Figure 5-1).

```
        4      6598 MCCLURE            986 OAK           LEI, IL        7832
7         300.00     525.00  1100.00 Memo
        9      2118 MOLANDER           1620 BROADWAY     SEATTLE, WA    9803
1         300.00     300.00  1000.00 Memo
        2      2145 MURPHY             23 OAK            LEI, IL        7832
7         150.00     157.50  4400.00 Memo
        8      6155 ODEGARD            2150 MAIN STREET  OAK, CA        9625
4         100.00     420.00  2750.00 Memo
Press any key to continue...
Record#  ACCT_NUM CUST_NAME           STREET            CITY_STATE     ZIP
         BEGIN_BAL UPDAT_BAL  CR_LIMIT TEXT
        1       411 TORREY             PO BOX 2          FIELDS, OR     9783
7         200.00     300.00  2000.00 Memo
(DEMO) . SEEK "TORREY"
(DEMO) . DELETE
      1 record deleted
(DEMO) . DISPLAY
Record#  ACCT_NUM CUST_NAME           STREET            CITY_STATE     ZIP
         BEGIN_BAL UPDAT_BAL  CR_LIMIT TEXT
        1 *     411 TORREY             PO BOX 2          FIELDS, OR     9783
7         200.00     300.00  2000.00 Memo
(DEMO) .
Command Line    <B:> MASTER                 Rec: 1/9              NumCaps
          Enter a dBASE III PLUS command.
```

Figure 5-1:   Record Marked for Deletion

The DELETE command can be used with modifiers. You can delete a
specific record by specifying its record number. As an exercise,
you will delete the first record in the database file.

Type **DELETE RECORD 1 [Enter]**
    Now two records are marked for deletion. You can see
    these with the following command.

Type **DISPLAY ALL ACCT_NUM, CUST_NAME [Enter]**
    Asterisks appear after the record numbers for TORREY and
    MURPHY, indicating the deleted records.

To unmark (that is, undelete) these records, you use the RECALL
command.

51

Type **RECALL ALL [Enter]**
　　　The message "2 records recalled" appears.

If you accidentally mark the wrong record for deletion, you can remove the asterisk by recalling the specific record number.

Delete Multiple Records

The DELETE command can also be used to select several records that meet a specific condition. Suppose you want to delete the records for all customers with an updated balance of 0.

Type **DELETE FOR UPDAT_BAL = 0 [Enter]**
　　　The message "2 records deleted" appears.

Type **LIST CUST_NAME, UPDAT_BAL [Enter]**
　　　This displays all the records and indicates with an asterisk that the records for customers HENDERSON and TORREY (those with UPDAT_BAL = 0) are marked for deletion.

As mentioned earlier, a database file may eventually contain many deleted records. You can physically remove them from the database file by packing the file.

Type **PACK [Enter]**
　　　The messages indicate that 7 records were copied and the indexes were rebuilt for the database file.

Type **LIST CUST_NAME, UPDAT_BAL [Enter]**
　　　The deleted records are no longer displayed. They no longer exist with the database file.

　　　When you pack a file, it is no longer possible to recover deleted records with the RECALL command. Thus, to physically delete records you must first mark them for deletion with the DELETE command, and then re-create your file, eliminating records marked for deletion with the PACK command.

Delete a File

The final example of removing records from a database file involves deleting all the records and packing the file. This can be done with a single command. When all the data in a database file is to be deleted and erased, but the file structure is to remain intact, then a single command, ZAP, deletes and packs the database file. An example is given in the following steps.

Type **ZAP [Enter]**
A message such as the following appears:

Zap A:\MASTER.dbf? (Y/N)

Type **Y** (do not press **[Enter]**)
Messages appear indicating that the indexes were rebuilt.

The status line indicates that there are no records in MASTER. If you should accidentally delete some or all records from MASTER, you can copy them from MASTERBU.

Type **APPEND FROM MASTERBU [Enter]**
A message indicates that 9 records were appended to MASTER.

Even though the physical records of the database file have changed, you can still use all the indexes you earlier built for MASTER.

You can continue or quit once you have completed this last operation of the lesson. If you decide to quit, remember to CLOSE ALL open files because failure to close the files before turning the computer off can result in lost of data!

Quick Review

You learned how to add records to your database file using APPEND. You also learned how to mark for deletion selected records from your database file using the DELETE command. The RECALL command was used to undelete records, and the PACK command was used to remove all the deleted records from the database file. The ZAP command was used to delete all the records from the database file and pack the file.

Summary

You have learned a number of methods for deletion. You have learned to delete a single record, multiple records, and all of the records in a file. In addition you have learned to delete the entire file including the file structure.

Review Questions

1. How can you remove an individual record?

2. How can you delete all records but retain the file structure?

3. How can you delete an entire file?

After completing this lesson, you will be able to:
o   **Join files to create another file**
o   **Create a report**
o   **Create a custom report format**

Joining Database Files

Separate files can be joined together to produce different combinations of tables. This resulting new file can include all the fields of the separate files or it can be a limited number of fields. This operation is similar to a wordprocessing activity of cut and paste to produce a new document.

The joining of two files with a common field will produce a third file. The DOT prompt command to accomplish the process is JOIN. Only those records with a common field in both files will appear in the new file.

All files that will be used in creating the new combination file must be loaded into memory. dBASE III PLUS allows you to store a file in each of ten work areas through the use of the SELECT command.

Join All Fields

In the following exercise you are to join together the MASTER and ARTRAN files to create a third file, ONEFILE. This new file will contain all the information about customers who were in both files.

Type **SELECT 1 [Enter]**
This creates the first work area.

Type **USE ARTRAN [Enter]**
    The ARTRAN file is loaded into work area 1.

Type **SELECT 2 [Enter]**
    The second work area is created.

Type **USE MASTER [Enter]**
    The MASTER file is loaded into memory.

Type **JOIN WITH ARTRAN TO ONEFILE FOR ACCT_NUM=ARTRAN->ACCT_NUM [Enter]**

To display the records in ONEFILE,

Type **USE ONEFILE [Enter]**
    The newly created file is now open and can be listed, displayed, and edited.

Type **BROWSE [Enter]**
    Use the [Home], [End], [Ctrl]-[→] and [Ctrl]-[←] keys to move back and forth between the fields of the records.

Press **[Esc]**
    You will be returned to the DOT prompt.

Join Selected Fields

You can create a file which is the result of combining only certain fields from other files. In this process you need to specify only those fields which are to be in the new file.

In this example you are to produce a file which contains only the ACCT_NUM, CUST_NAME, CITY_STATE, REF_NO, and AMOUNT fields. Because ARTRAN is still in work area 1 you do not need to repeat the SELECT command. However, you do need to bring MASTER file into memory to replace ONEFILE from the previous exercise.

Type **USE MASTER [Enter]**

Type **JOIN WITH ARTRAN TO TWOFILE FOR ACCT_NUM=ARTRAN->ACCT_NUM FIELDS ACCT_NUM, CUST_NAME, CITY_STATE, REF_NO, AMOUNT [Enter]**
    The new file is created with only the specified fields. To examine the records in the new file,

Type **USE TWOFILE [Enter]**

Type **BROWSE [Enter]**
    This new file contains only the specified fields and can now be accessed to be printed in a report.

Press **[Esc]**
>   Returns to the DOT prompt mode. If the TWOFILE file is
>   not going to be used at this time or you are quitting,
>   close all files.

Creating Reports

You can group related data together with a report. You have the
capability to print fields where you want them and perform
calculations on those fields also. Reports allow you to retrieve
and manipulate your database data according to your own special
needs. You will use TWOFILE.DBF. file to create a report. After
you have created, saved, and displayed the report, you will learn
how to print it.

Report Format - Page Heading

Use the following steps to create a report format for the TWOFILE
file:

1. Type **C** to move to Create in the main menu, position the
    selection bar on **Report**, and press **[Enter]**.

2. Select drive **A** and press **[Enter]**.

3. At the prompt of "Enter the name of the file:" type **TEST**.

4. With the selection bar on **Page title**, press **[Enter]**.

5. Type: **Monthly Customer Report**, press **[PgDn]**.

6. Position the selection bar on **Right margin** and press **[Enter]**.
    Type **2** and press **[Enter]**. This gives you two spaces on the
    right margin.

7. Position the selection bar on **Page eject before printing** and
    press **[Enter]**. The Yes will turn to a No automatically.

8. Position the selection bar on **Page eject after printing** and
    press **[Enter]**. The No will turn to a Yes automatically.

Report Format - Columns

9. Use the [→] key to move the highlight bar to the **Columns**
    choice in the menu.

10. With the selection bar on **Contents**, press **[Enter]**. Press **[F10]** to use the file structure field names in a menu. Position the selection bar on **ACCT_NUM** and press **[Enter]** twice.

11. Move selection bar down one row to **Heading** and press **[Enter]**.

12. Type the report column heading: **ACCT NO.** and press **[PgDn]** twice.

13. Repeat steps 10 to 12 for each of the following fields: ACCT_NUM, CUST_NAME, CITY_STATE, REF_NO, and AMOUNT.

14. After the final column is specified, move the top row highlight to **Exit** and press **[Enter]** with the selection bar on **Save**.

The report format will now be saved as TEST file and can be retrieved any time you want to print the report.

Report Format - Retrieving

After the database has been brought into the current memory, the report format for printing can be retrieved. Not only will the report format be followed in the printing but it will also appear in the same format on the screen.

Use the Report created in the previous example to print a report using the TWOFILE file.

1. Type **R** to move to the Retrieve command in the main menu, position the selection bar at the **Report** option, and press **[Enter]**.

2. Select drive **A** and press **[Enter]**.

3. Select **TEST** on the menu and press **[Enter]**.

4. With the selection bar on the **Execute the command** option, press **[Enter]**.

5. At the prompt of "Send the output to the printer? [Y/N]," type **Y**.

The output will appear on the screen (Figure. 6-1) as well as at the printer.

You can continue or quit once you have completed this last operation of the lesson. If you decide to quit, remember to CLOSE ALL open files because failure to close the files before turning

the computer off can result in lost of data! Quit dBASE III PLUS
in the Setup menu automatically closes the open files.

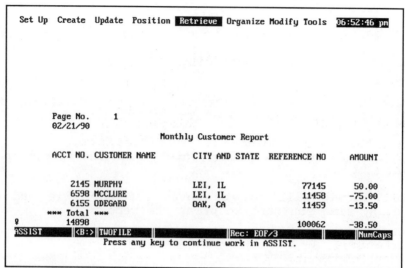

Figure 6-1:   Printed Report Form

Summary

In this final exercise you have joined two database files together
to form a third file which contained some or all of the data from
the original two files. To make the new file useful, you created
a Report Form to be used in the printing of the data in the third
file. The Report Form was saved and could be retrieved for later
use.

This lesson concludes the tutorial of the most commonly used
features of dBASE III PLUS.

REVIEW QUESTIONS

1.   What must two or more files have in common when they are
     joined to form yet another file?

2.   The SELECT command can be used to create how many work areas?

3.   When printing a report from a file, not only can you have the
     fields printed where you want them, but what else can you do
     to the data before it is printed?

INDEX

Append 15
    Browse 47
Arithmetic 38
ASSIST 6

Backup Copy 18

Database File
    Create 12, 16
    Join 54
    Retrieve 21, 28
    Saving 19
dBASE III PLUS
    ASSIST 2, 6
    DOT 2
    DOT Prompt 6
    Exit 7
    Limitations 3
    Screen Components 4
    Starting 3
Delete
    File 52
    Files 50
    Multiple Records 52
    Records 50
    Single Record 50
Display
    All Records 29
    Record Field
        Structure 28
    Selected Fields 30
    Selected Records 30
DOT Prompt 6

Edit 49
    Browse 48
    Record Contents 23

FIELD 13
    Decimal 13
    FIELD NAME 13
    TYPE 13
    WIDTH 13
Files
    Deleting 50
    Sort 40, 42
Function Keys 6

Help 10
History 39

Index
    Create 43
    Retrieving 46
Join
    All Fields 54
    Database Files 54
    Selected Fields 55

List
    Records 25
    Specific Fields 26
    Specific Records 26

Modify 21
    Add a field 21
    File Record Structure 22

Record Field Structure
    Display 15
Records
    Deleting 50
Replace
    Fields 35
    Records 34
Report
    Format 56
Reports
    Create 56

Sort
    Multiple Fields 41
    Single field 40
Statistical function
    AVERAGE 37
    COUNT 37
    SUM 37